MANCHESTER
a new look

Willow
PUBLISHING KEITH WARRENDER

Manchester a New Look
© 2002 Willow Publishing
© Photography Keith Warrender
unless named contributor

Published by Willow Publishing
Willow Cottage, 36 Moss Lane,
Timperley, Altrincham,
Cheshire WA15 6SZ

Printed by
Buxton Press Ltd

ISBN 0 946361 39 8

In memory of my father

Above:
The Lowry and
HMS Bronington,
The Quays

Left:
Manchester
Central Library,
St Peter's Square

Title page:
Urbis Museum

Contents

Above:
Dovestones Reservoir
Saddleworth

Opposite page:
City of Manchester Stadium
John Rylands Library
Whitworth Art Gallery
Great Northern Square

Introduction

The City of Manchester has seen significant change in recent years and many areas have a new look. Attractive open spaces have been created in the City centre such as Great Northern Square, Exchange Square and Manchester's first new park for many years - Cathedral Gardens. Piccadilly, one of the City's focal points, with the fountains and landscaped area, is a popular place to relax. New buildings such as the towering Urbis and Number One Deansgate blocks have transformed the skyline. The enormous growth of new flats, offices and hotel developments, as well as warehouse conversions has seen whole streets completely changed and renewed. Manchester has become a place where increasing numbers of people want to live to add to its role as an important centre for commerce, shopping, sport, entertainment, education, the

arts and media. The City and the surrounding area has become an attractive place to explore and to spend time and this was reflected in Manchester being the host for the Commonwealth Games. Greater Manchester has plenty to offer the visitor and its residents with so many heritage sites, countryside attractions and visitor centres. This new look at the area gives a glimpse of some of these places. You may be surprised at the range of wonderful things to see and do around Greater Manchester. The book starts with Manchester's squares and then looks around the City centre in a roughly clock-wise direction. It then moves to places within the City boundaries and close by, before taking another clock-wise sweep across Greater Manchester and other popular visitor destinations just outside the area.

Above: Luxury apartments overlooking Parsonage Gardens off Deansgate

Right: St Peter's Square
Imperial War Museum North
King Street

Opposite page
Inset: Number One Deansgate and the Royal Exchange from Market Street
Below: Cross Street, looking towards Urbis museum

Around the City

Albert Square

The pedestrianised square is dominated by the Albert Memorial (right) designed by Thomas Worthington and completed in 1867.

The Thirlmere fountain, also by Worthington, was erected here in 1897 to celebrate the completion of the water supply from the Lake District and also the Diamond Jubilee of Queen Victoria. Later it was re-erected in Heaton Park but it was restored and returned to its original site in 1998.

Other statues in the Square are of John Bright - Quaker Statesman, Gladstone - Prime Minister, Oliver Heywood - banker and benefactor, and the second Bishop of Manchester - Thomas Woolner.

Above: St George's Day Parade

Left: St Mary's RC Church, a haven of peace in the busy City, is just off the Square in Mulberry Street. Built in 1848 on the site of an earlier chapel, it is known as 'The Hidden Gem' and is noted for the impressive altar which includes life-size saints and angel figures

Above left: *Albert Square* **Above right:** *Lincoln Square with the statue of the American President given by the USA in 1919, in recognition of the support given by the Lancashire cotton weavers and spinners towards the Union cause in the Civil War and the abolition of slavery*

Left: *St George's Day dragon, Albert Square.* **Above:** *Italy Festival*

Opposite page, top: Manchester Town Hall, designed by Alfred Waterhouse and opened in 1877. Described as 'Manchester's Civic Cathedral' it is one of the finest civic buildings in England

Left: Manchester's Albert Memorial was built before the London monument and was designed by Thomas Worthington

Below: Brazennose Street and Lincoln Square

European Christmas market, Albert Square

Right: The tower of Manchester Town Hall is over 280 feet high and houses 24 bells. The great hour bell is said to be the largest perfect clock bell in England

Three of six statues on the Albert Square, Princess Street corner of the Town Hall - (left to right) John Bradford, Protestant martyr during the reign of Queen Mary, Thomas de la Warr, founder of the Collegiate Church, Thomas Grelle, the Lord of the manor who granted the 'great charter of Manchester' in 1301

The Albert Square entrance with the statue of chemist and philosopher John Dalton.
Above is a circular trap door to enable the bells to be lowered from the tower

Manchester Town Hall

Left: The Great Hall with the ceiling showing many of Manchester's international trading partners. On the walls are twelve murals by Ford Madox Brown depicting key incidents in Manchester's history. They took 15 years to paint and were finished in 1893. The organ, by Monsieur Cavaille-Coll of Paris, was installed in 1877

Above top: The Conference Room with oak screen, canopy and gallery was originally the Council Chamber

Above: James Joule statue by Alfred Gilbert in the main entrance. Joule discovered the mechanical equivalent of heat and a 'joule' is now a recognised electrical unit

Manchester Town Hall

Facing page: One of the two grand staircases leading to the Great Hall

Above top: Ford Madox Brown mural - 'The Expulsion of the Danes in 910'

Above: A triptych of Sir John Barbirolli, conductor of the Halle Orchestra, in the Sculpture Hall

Right: Town Hall rear entrance, Cooper Street

Below left: Detail from the mosaic landing. The bee is symbolic of Manchester's industry and is on the coat of arms

Below right: Staircase to landing

The square is named after the church which stood here until it was demolished in 1907 and replaced by a Memorial Cross (left) designed by Temple Moore. The garden and the Cenotaph War Memorial by Sir Edward Lutyens were added in 1924.

The Midland Hotel opened in 1903 for the Midland Railway Company. It has the distinction of being the only hotel in England to have its own postmark.

Central library and the Town Hall Extension were both designed by E Vincent Harris. The design of the Library which opened in 1934, was inspired by the Pantheon in Rome. The Town Hall Extension opened four years later.

To the north of the Square is the Peace Gardens with a peace sculpture (below) designed by Barbara Pearson in 1986. The trees in the garden have been donated by different countries.

Near the Library are the figures 'Struggle For Peace and Freedom' by Philip Jackson, 1988.

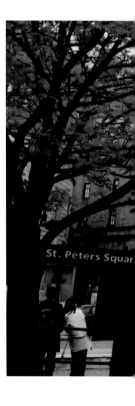

St Peter's Square

The Town Hall Extension with the Peace garden on the left

The Central Library has a spectacular domed reading room. After winning the competition to design the library, architect Vincent Harris toured the United States to research the latest trends in library design. The Library's 20 miles of shelves house many collections. In the basement is the Library Theatre - one of the earliest civic theatres - and used as a BBC studio during the last War.

When Marlene Dietrich visited the Midland Hotel in 1965, she refused the deserts on the menu and asked for a jam omelette!

Central Library - visited by over one and a half million people each year

The Central Library was officially opened by King George V and Queen Mary in 1934 and despite being called 'the Civic Egg Box' during construction, it remains one of Britain's busiest libraries and a City landmark

Great Northern Square

This new square, bounded by Deansgate and Peter Street, was opened in 1999, on the site of the goods yard for the Great Northern Company's Warehouse. Beneath the five floors of the warehouse, built in 1898, there was an interchange of road and railway for the Manchester and Salford Junction Canal. The converted warehouse and adjoining new buildings now contain a cinema, gym, shops, restaurants and bars. In the square there is an outdoor performance amphitheatre.

Right: The tall white building is Sunlight House, built by Joe Sunlight in 1932. He was a Russian refugee who became one of this country's biggest property developers. His friends Douglas Fairbanks Jnr and Dorothy Lamour opened the building, which was the tallest in Europe at the time, and the first high rise block in Manchester

Below: The tower behind the square is the former Methodist Church - Albert Hall. It was a centre of temperance, in contrast to the present day establishment which promotes itself as a place for 'eating, dancing and cavorting'

St Ann's Square

The square was a cornfield and the site of the annual three day fair in Manchester from 1222, known as Acres Field. By 1823 it had become a fashionable, tree-lined, shopping area and residential area, and the fair with all its livestock was moved to Knott Mill.

An Act of Parliament in 1708 authorised the building of St Ann's Church (seen in the background), with the instructions that thirty yards had to be left clear in front of the church to enable the fair to continue.

It is thought that the church was built for attenders at the Collegiate Church who wanted a simpler form of worship. The new church was consecrated in 1712 and financed by Lady Ann Bland, one of the Mosley family, lords of the Manor, who lived at Hulme Hall. Lady Bland performed the laying of the foundation stone ceremony in 1709. John Byrom, writer of the Christmas hymn 'Christians Awake', was a member of the congregation.

The church now plays a big part in city life with midday services, special services and recitals. Its rectors are occasionally Chaplains to the Lord Mayor.

In the foreground is a memorial to the Boer War - a rifleman protecting his comrade - erected in 1907.

Left: Fountain in St Ann's Square
by P Randall-Page, 1996

Right: St Ann's Church from the
back. It was built in purple-red
Collyhurst sandstone in the
Renaissance style of Sir Christopher
Wren, but it was more probably the
work of local builder and architect
John Barker

Below right: The view from the
church tower looks beyond the
Square to Manchester's newest
street - aptly named New Cathedral
Street - which provides a through
pedestrian link to Manchester
Cathedral. The dome on the right
is the Royal Exchange building

Left: The back of St Ann's Church **Above top:** *Argo and the Golden fleece
sculpture on the former Manchester Liners offices* **Above:** *Barton Arcade*

St Ann's Church

Painted glass window by William Peckitt of York, 1768. He made stained glass for royalty and his work is to be seen in many buildings

The fine Georgian oak pulpit has been lowered beneath floor level in order to be less dominating. John Wesley visited here between 1733 and 1738

There have been several major internal renovations over the years, including work, by Alfred Waterhouse, who raised the level of the chancel and sanctuary and enclosed them with a low wrought-iron screen. Later redecoration has enhanced the Georgian mouldings bordering the ceiling

Above middle: X.trax Street Festival around St Ann's Square **Below:** German Christmas Market in the Square

Right: The Barton Arcade off St Ann's Square, built in 1871, Manchester's only surviving Victorian arcade and one of the finest examples of a cast-iron and glass-roofed arcade in the country

The Royal Exchange

The Royal Exchange was once the centre of the world's cotton industry. It had the world's largest trading floor and had up to 11,000 members representing the textile industry. Trading took place twice a week and the prices from the final day in 1968 are still displayed (see below).

Earlier exchange buildings on this site dating from 1874 had been used for large meetings and even theatrical performances. It was perhaps not too surprising that after a few years of disuse, the building became the site for a temporary theatre, followed by a permanent structure completed in 1976.

Beneath the three domes is an impressive glass and tubular-steel theatre-in-the-round construction with 750 seats. Within the hall there are also a studio theatre, cafe, craft centre and bookshop.

The Royal Exchange Theatre Company presents a wide range of productions ranging from the traditional to new radical works. Many well known actors have appeared here, including Tom Courtenay, Albert Finney and Vanessa Redgrave

Exchange Square

A new public space has been created in front of the building previously known as the Corn Exchange. The interior has been transformed into elegant retail units and renamed *The Triangle*.

The square has become a popular meeting place and is dominated by a line of tilting windmills (opposite).

The water feature traces the possible line of the watercourse called Hanging Ditch which was culverted in the 17th century.

Right: *This postbox on Cross Street just off Exchange Square, withstood the biggest ever terrorist bomb on mainland Britain in 1996, which devastated part of the city centre. The hundred year old post box protected its contents, and after being removed for the rebuilding of Marks and Spencer, it was returned to its original site in 1999*

The Triangle, Exchange Square

Above: The Triangle shopping centre **Right:** The Printworks
entertainment centre with cinemas, shops, bars and restaurants

Urbis

Urbis Museum which opened in 2002 explores life in different cities of the world. Visitors begin their visit with a ride up the Glass Elevator and then look round the four floors of themed exhibitions entitled - *Arrive*, *Change*, *Order* and *Explore*. Exhibits are interactive and use the latest technology for experiences such as a virtual taxi ride through Singapore, and a helicopter trip over Sao Paolo.

Cathedral Gardens, (left) next to Urbis, is Manchester's first new public park in 70 years, surrounded by the Triangle and Chetham's School of Music.

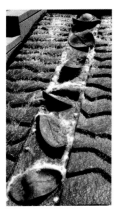

Waterfall, Cathedral Gardens

The Old Wellington Inn and Sinclair's Oyster Bar are known as The Shambles. They have been moved from their original site and reformed in an L-shape. The work was completed in 1999. The 16th century Old Wellington Inn was the birthplace of John Byrom, hymn writer and inventor of phonetic shorthand. It only became a public house in 1830 and was known as the Vintners Arms. The Byrom family owned both properties for around 250 years.

Sinclairs is one of the oldest chop houses and oyster bars in the country. During preservation work some years ago, an oak beam was discovered dated 1328 and workmen also found a wall built of willow and cemented with cow dung and hair. John

Shaw became the owner in 1738 and established a 'Punch House'. He was a military man and ran the place accordingly. It was a popular venue for local traders who would enjoy sixpennyworth of punch and two pipes of tobacco, but he insisted it should close at 8pm. Anyone still lingering after that time would see Shaw holding a whip with a long lash, calling out 'Past eight o'clock, gentlemen!' The rule was enforced by his servant Molly, who would start mopping the floors. The punch was served in two sizes of china bowls known as 'Pees' and 'Kews' for a shilling or sixpence and Molly would have warned them to mind their 'P's and Q's'. Lady Spittlewick was a regular customer for oysters, consuming forty daily. One day she was taken ill and died in hospital - she had choked on a pearl!

Above left: Guided tour near the Cathedral. *Above right:* Thomas Minshull, apothecary, bequeathed this property on Cateaton Street, dated 1689, to give employment to 'poor, sound and healthy' boys of the City. *Opposite:* Manchester Cathedral

Sator Rotas Stone* which was found during the excavation of the Roman Fort and is the earliest evidence of Christianity in Britain. It dates from around AD185 and can be read in four directions. If rearranged in the form of a cross it reads PATERNOSTER - 'Our Father' - the first words of the Lord's Prayer

*The original is held at Manchester Museum

The Cathedral Visitor Centre

The Centre contains Hanging Bridge (above) which dates from 1415, and has been hidden from view under the raised street level for over 300 years. The bridge connected the old church to the medieval town over a dip called Hanging Ditch. Other treasures on view are a replica of the Sator Rotas Stone (left) and a replica fragment of John's Gospel*, dated within 100 years of Christ's death and less than 50 years after the gospel was first written. There are 'virtual reality' tours of the Cathedral, displays about the Cathedral's history and in an interactive section where visitors can use computers to compose their own song for the choir.

* The original fragment is at John Rylands Library- see page 103

50

Manchester Cathedral

There has probably been a church here since the 8th century. Records of the early church were lost when they were taken to London around 1650 and destroyed by the Great Fire in 1666. In 1421 Henry V granted a Royal Charter to Thomas de la Warre of the manor of Manchester to found the Collegiate Church. The present church is the third on this site and mainly built in the 15th century in the Perpendicular style. It is the widest mediaeval church in Britain and became a Cathedral in 1847.

*Mother and Child
by Charles Wheeler*

Eric Gill Sculpture, 1933

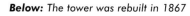

Below: *The tower was rebuilt in 1867*

The Choir (right) has thirty canopied stalls installed around 1500. They depict mediaeval scenes and legends and are fine examples of craftsmanship with carvings of eagles, dragons, lions, monkeys and unicorns on the bench ends and underneath the seats

The Cathedral suffered badly in the bombing of the last World War, including the destruction of the stained glass windows, but they have been replaced by the work of Antony Hollaway.

Above: The Choir Screen is a great example of mediaeval wood carving

Far left: The Bishop's Throne was made in 1906. 'Cathedra' is from the Greek word for chair. Therefore if a church is to be a Cathedral it has to have one of these

Left: The 'Angel Stone' is an 8th century fragment from a Saxon church. The inscription on it reads 'Into thy hands, O Lord, I commend my spirit'

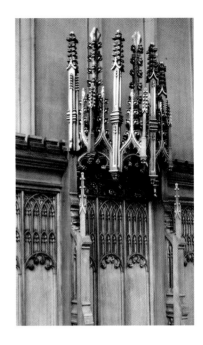

Above: 'Revelation' produced in 1995, one of Antony Hollaway's stained glass designs. In front is the statue of Humphrey Chetham, who founded the boys' school next to the cathedral. The school has since become a noted school of music for boys and girls

Right: Examples of the carved seats - known as 'pity seats' - in the Choir which allowed the clergy some respite while standing through long services.
Top: The 15th century Chapter House, used on formal occasions

The Northern Quarter

This page:
Manchester Craft and Design Centre is based in the 1890 fish and poultry market. Designers and craftspeople both produce and sell their work here

Opposite page:
Farmers' Market outside the former Wholesale Fish Market, off High Street

OPENED · 14 · FEB · 1873 · BOOTH · MAYOR

HIGH STREET

AND PERHAPS THESE PAVEMENT CRACKS ARE THE PLACES WHERE WEARY WORKERS CONGEEATED

Opposite page: 'Tib Street Horn' by David Kemp
Top left: 'A New Broom' by George Wylie
Above: Ceramic birds, Tib Street reminding us this was a popular area for pet shops
Left: Market, Church Street

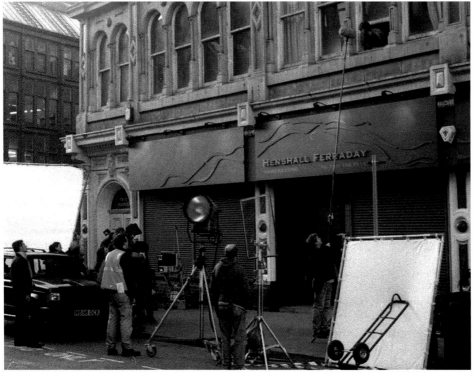

Left: Cafe Pop, Oldham Street

Opposite and below: Affleck's Palace

Below left: Filming in the Northern Quarter for the BBC drama production 'Cutting It'

Greater Manchester Police Museum is situated in a former Victorian Police Station on Newton Street. There are riot gates, a charge office and cell block along with displays which trace the history of the police service. Rare relics include a truncheon and banner from the time of the Peterloo Massacre, and a cosh and pistol belonging to a Victorian detective

Left: Occupants on solid wooden pillows in the Victorian cells

Below: The Station's Charge Office

The City Pub on Oldham Street **(above)** has a plasterwork panel on the frontage showing William and Mary arriving in England greeted by Britannia, a clergyman and an angel. The pub was known as 'The Prince of Orange' in 1800

Artisans' houses on Bradley Street are the only surviving one-up one-down houses in the centre of Manchester. They were built in 1787, to the rear of grander properties on Lever Street, and as many as twelve people lived in each house. The row was rebuilt in 1996 and is Grade 2 Listed

The Daily Express building which dominates Great Ancoats Street, was designed by Sir Owen Williams in 1939, following similar offices in London and Glasgow. The printing presses were in the triple-height press hall

Piccadilly Gardens

The old sunken gardens have been transformed into a new public space, linked with surrounding pedestrian routes by a new catwalk bridge. Around a hundred new trees have been planted and the spectacular water feature, which uses fibre optic lighting, is an impressive sight at night.

Top and Left: The Britannia Hotel on Portland Street used to be Watts Warehouse. It was the largest in the City when it opened in 1851 and each floor was given a distinctive look. The ground floor is in the Egyptian style, with higher floors decorated in the Italian, French Renaissance and Elizabethan manner. Charles Dickens described the warehouse as 'the Merchant Palace of Europe'. There is an impressive staircase and memorials to employees who lost their lives during the two World Wars. The Hotel opened in 1982.

Above: The Circus Tavern, Portland Street, is Manchester's smallest pub where there is room for just one person behind the bar. The Tavern was built about 1790 and it was named after a nearby Circus on Chatham Street. The Portland Street area used to attract travelling circuses and the tavern was one of several establishments which was used by both entertainers and customers from the shows. The pub's woodgrained partitions are around 100 years old.

Top right: Mosley Street

66

Manchester Art Gallery

The Gallery on Mosley Street opened in 1882 and has now been extended to link with the Athenaeum, a former gentleman's club, on Princess Street, and a new building on Nicholas Street. The Mosley Street building was designed by Charles Barry - architect of the Houses of Parliament. The Gallery has a fine collection of Pre-Raphaelite paintings, special exhibitions of contemporary work, themed shows relating to Manchester and a gallery of craft and design with 1,300 objects. There is also space for local people to have their work displayed and an interactive gallery of special interest to children.

Above left: 'Work' by Ford Madox Brown which took 13 years to complete in 1865

Above right: 'Laying a Foundation Stone' by L S Lowry 1936

The Library was visited by many eminent people from the literary world, including Elizabeth Gaskell and Thomas de Quincey. John Dalton received honorary membership in exchange for winding up the clock. It has a collection of 25,000 books, mainly works from the19th century. **Below right:** William Gaskell, Chairman 1849-1884

The Portico Library & Gallery

It was founded by a group of Manchester men, and modelled on the Liverpool Lyceum. It opened as a Library and Newsroom which were on the ground floor and now occupies the first floor of the building. Peter Mark Roget, who compiled the famous Thesaurus was the first Secretary. Today everything is housed under the magnificent domed ceiling, and there is a varied lecture and exhibition programme.

Chinatown

The area developed its distinctive character in the 1970's as the Chinese community moved into the empty warehouses to open restaurants. Now it is a centre with supermarkets, and medicine and craft shops which attract many people. The Chinese New Year is celebrated with parties and a dancing dragon which moves around the streets.

69

The Chinese Imperial Arch on Faulkner Street was built in 1987 - the first of its kind in Europe. It was put together by 12 specialist craftworkers from Beijing, and is considered the most important in this country because of its size and scale. It is the focal point of Chinatown and for the Chinese New Year festivities

Around Whitworth Street

Above left: *Archimedes by Thompson W Dagnall, on the UMIST campus*
Above right: *The Palace Hotel*
Below: *Alan Turing memorial in Sackville Gardens*

Above: *A Monument to Vimto by Kerry Morrison, 1992. The first batch of the product was produced here in Granby Row in 1908*
Below: *Chorlton Street*

Opposite page:

Alan Turing *1912-1954 was a mathematician and expert in many subjects and is credited with developing the device which broke the famous Enigma Code during World War II. He has been described as 'the founder of computer science', and while in Manchester contributed to the building and program-ming of the first all-electronic computers*

Sackville Gardens *was created on land acquired in the 1880's to stop new building obstructing the view of the School of Technology, now called UMIST, which opened in 1902*

The Palace Hotel, *on the corner of Oxford Road and Whitworth Street, was previously offices for the Refuge Assurance Company and designed in 1891 by Alfred Waterhouse. The clocktower is 220 feet high. The substantial basements were used by the 1300 employees as an air raid shelter during the Second World War*

Left:
Lancaster House and its 'wedding cake tower' was completed in1910 in the Edwardian Baroque style by leading architect in warehouse design - Harry S Fairhurst

Left: The Palace Hotel seen from Oxford Street

Top left: The Palace Theatre on Oxford Street which first opened in 1891. It is now a venue for lavish musicals, dance companies and pantomime

Top right: The Corner House on Oxford Road has three galleries showing contemporary art, photography and sculpture. It also has three cinemas, a shop, bar and cafe

Right: Deansgate Locks on the Rochdale Canal, Whitworth Street West, where there are bars and a comedy club. There are six miles of canals and rivers running through the centre of the City

Opposite page
Top: *Peveril of the Peak*
on Bridgewater Street.
It was tiled around 1900
Below left: *Bike sculpture*
'The Cycle of Life' 1994,
next to Knott Mill Station

Left and above:
Deansgate Locks
Top and right:
Bridgewater Hall

Bridgewater Hall

The Hall is the base for the Halle Orchestra, the BBC
Philharmonic and the Manchester Camerata. It opened
in 1996 and is the first of its kind to be built in the UK
since the Royal Festival Hall in 1951. It also has the
largest mechanical pipe organ to be installed in the UK
in the 20th century. The auditorium, which seats 2,400,
is supported on springs which
cushion the noise and vibrations
from passing traffic and trams.

*Sir John Barbirolli (right) was the
Halle's most distinguished Principal
Conductor. He led the Orchestra
from 1943 right up to his death
in 1969, having established its
international status*

Above: *The Midland Hotel* **Below:** *Rochdale Canal Basin below Barbirolli Square*

Above: The G-Mex Centre and Manchester International Convention Centre

Above: *Soon after it opened, the Midland (now the Crowne Plaza) was the City's leading hotel. There were banqueting rooms, concerts in the roof gardens, electric lighting and communications that made it possible to make reservations in mid Atlantic. It also had its own theatre as well as 400 'bed chambers, each with a clock and coal fire'. It was here, in 1904, that Charles Rolls met with local businessman Frederick Royce to form the soon-to-be famous motor company*

Below: *Curved marble pebble by Kan Yasuda 1996 in front of buildings in Barbirolli Square*

G-Mex - Greater Manchester Exhibition Centre

It was formerly Central Station (left), Manchester's fourth terminal from 1880, until it closed in 1969. Destinations from here included London St Pancras, the 'hikers' special' to the Peak District and the well-run 43 minute service to Liverpool. It reopened in its present form in 1986 and its unsupported arch span of 64 metres creates 10,000 metres of potential exhibition space.

Castlefield

Castlefield, named after the Roman fort here, is Britain's first Urban Heritage Park. Today it is a popular area to visit, with canalside walks, cafes, bars, refurbished warehouses and a Roman fort. The Bridgewater and Rochdale canals meet at this point close to the Merchants Bridge (above) constructed in 1996. The Duke of Bridgewater built his canal

in 1761 to bring coal from his collieries at Worsley. James Brindley, one of the engineers of the first modern canal, ensured a quick journey by following the contours of the route, rather than using time-consuming locks. The Rochdale canal, completed in 1805, was the first waterway over the Pennines.

Above: The Duke's Pub was originally a stable block for the canal horses working around the wharfs and named after the adjacent 92nd lock. The Rochdale Canal was a busy waterway, starting at Sowerby Bridge, with around 50 narrowboats using it daily. Tolls were collected here as it joined up with the Bridgewater Canal

Opposite page: Barca, a Spanish theme bar, Catalan Square

The annual Castlefield Carnival is centred on the
canal basin near Liverpool Road, in the outdoor arena

The red brick tower is a former Congregational chapel which has been converted into a recording studio and basement cafe. Other features here include the rebuilt Grocers' Warehouse (below left), where coal was hauled up to Castle Street, red sandstone cliffs and a local radio station

The Museum of Science and Industry

The Museum, on Liverpool Road, includes the world's oldest passenger railway station from the 1830's and is full of galleries with hands-on exhibits and working machinery, covering the history and development of Manchester. There are exhibitions about the cotton industry, computer technology and space science.

In the Power Hall (this page) is the world's largest collection of working steam engines and locally built cars, motorbikes and trains.

Above: Sycamore helicopter

The Air and Space Hall at The Museum of Science and Industry has the largest collection of aircraft in the North West. It is housed in the old food market of 1876.

Above: Replica of the Roe triplane made in 1909. Its longest flight was just 120' - the wingspan of the Shackleton (right)

Above: An Avro 707 -
a Vulcan experimental plane

Left: 'Dougal' the world's
best preserved Shackleton

Below:
Japanese suicide bomb
Model of the SS Enterprise

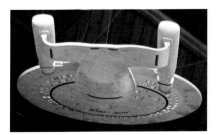

Above: The First Class Booking Hall and platform at Liverpool Road - the world's first passenger station

Right top: Roman fort reconstruction of the North Gate, built in 1986. The Mamucium fort was established in 79 AD by General Agricola with 500 soldiers and civilian support. The Romans withdrew in 400 AD but the civilian settlement remained. The remains of the fort were visible in the 18th century and the area was known as 'Castle-in-the-Field'

Right: The set of Coronation Street, in 1990 - the world's longest running television soap opera

Below: The White Lion Pub is next to the foundations of the civilian buildings and a Roman garden

Right: The pub is named after Mark Addy who, while helping with his father's boat-hire business, rescued over 50 people from the murky River Irwell. His last rescue was in 1889 and he was awarded the Albert Medal for his bravery by Queen Victoria, and the grateful people of Salford gave him 500 guineas

Below: The Pump House, home of the People's History Museum, on the banks of the River Irwell, opened in 1909. It is Manchester's last remaining Hydraulic Pumping Station, which helped to provide power for local cotton mills, winding up the Town Hall clock and raising the Opera House's safety Curtain

Doves of Peace, Bridge Street
by Michael Lyons, 1986

The People's History Museum

The Museum, off Bridge Street, is devoted to lives of ordinary people, focussing on the labour organisations that brought about change. It looks at the workplace, home-life and how people enjoyed themselves. The displays feature life in Manchester - the first industrial city, radical reformers for a fairer, more democratic society, early trade societies, including rural activity such as the Tolpuddle Martyrs, socialism, women's suffrage, co-operative societies, and Labour politics.

Left: The five star Lowry Hotel (left) and the Trinity Bridge, linking Manchester with Salford, by Santiago Calatrava, completed 1995.

Above: Victoria Bridge replaced a 14th century structure which had a dungeon for drunks. Blackfriars Bridge, in the background, was completed in 1820, replacing a wooden footbridge built in 1761 by a group of comedy actors to attract people over to their theatre in Salford. The once heavily polluted River Irwell is now a haven for fish and wild life. Chubb, bass and roach are found here, and brown trout have been sighted further up river. Anglers who like to fish here have seen swans and kingfishers.

Deansgate

No 1 Deansgate (above and left) is a new prestigious block of luxury apartments supported by slender silver 'Y' pillars. The design - conceived as a simple glass prism - slopes down to the Cathedral and up to the City. The building is also Manchester's biggest barometer because the windows are fitted with sensors and will automatically close if it rains. So, if you see the louvred windows start to close, from top to bottom on the building - it's time to put up your umbrella.

Above: John Rylands Library - Manchester's 'Taj Mahal' (see page 102)
Below: The 'streaky bacon' style Deansgate facade of the Great Northern Railway Goods Warehouse

Around Deansgate

Manchester's wide range of bars and restaurants is reflected in the *Good food Guide* in which the City has most entries in the regions

Above: *Kendal Milne's department store, built 1939. The original store was in the building opposite*

This page, middle: *The former Free Library on the corner of Deansgate and Liverpool Road, built in1882, now a restaurant and Spanish language and cultural centre*

Opposite page, bottom: *Parsonage Gardens - possibly the site of a priest's house in Saxon times. Later it became the churchyard belonging to 18th century St Mary's Church, which closed in 1890*

John Rylands Library

The metalwork is early art nouveau style in a building which was one of the first to be lit by electricity - cleaner and safer than gas

Mrs Rylands founded the library in 1900 in memory of her husband. It took ten years to build and is one of the finest examples of Gothic architecture in Europe. John Rylands was a cotton merchant, and when he died he left a fortune, which his widow used on the building and acquiring a library collection which is one of the best in the country. No expense was spared, both on the architectural design, the fixtures, fittings and furniture, and the purchase of important collections of printed books, and western and oriental manuscripts.

Right: Fragment of John's Gospel

Below left: Statues representing Theology directing the labours of Science and the Arts

Below and top left: The walls and the stained glass in the Reading Room have the figures of sixty learned men, to inspire scholars. The white statues of John and Enriqueta Rylands stand at either end of the room

Opposite right: St John's Gardens, Byrom Street, are named after the churchyard on this site. William Marsden, buried here, was the first to give his workers Saturday afternoons off in 1843. Charlotte Bronte is said to have started writing Jane Eyre here. There is a gravestone for John Owens, founder of Owens College on Quay Street. He died in 1846 and left £96,000 for 'instructing and improving young persons of the male sex'. The College opened with a staff of seven in 1851 and became a University in 1881

Opposite, below: St John Street - Manchester's 'Harley Street' with many medical consultants prcticing here. It is the best surviving Georgian terrace in the centre of Manchester built between 1770 and 1830. The leading merchants lived here in the mid 18th century, when it marked the edge of the town's built -up area

Left: The Opera House on Quay Street, formerly known as the New Theatre and built in1912, is a venue for touring West End musicals

Above: Window and 'Gothic' door, Byrom Street

Opposite:
Manchester Town Hall
from St Ann's Church tower

This page:
Left and bottom: King Street
Middle left: Cross Street
Middle right: Mr Thomas's
Chop House, Cross Street
dated 1901

The former Brook's Bank, Brown Street 1868.
To the right is the 'King of King Street' - the impressive
Midland Bank by Sir Edward Lutyens, 1935

The Reform Club, (on left) at the top of King Street,
dated 1870, where Winston Churchill greeted
celebrating crowds from the balcony, after the
Liberal's General Election victory in 1906

Above: The Shakespeare pub, Fountain
Street, which was rebuilt in 1923 using
sections from an old Chester building

Left: Office block behind the former Bank
of England on King Street

Chetham's Library

It was founded in 1653, on Long Millgate, and is the oldest surviving public library in the English speaking world. Humphrey Chetham was a wealthy Manchester merchant who endowed it in his will, along with a hospital school which is now Chetham's School of Music. The Library building dates from 1421 and was used as a college of priests to serve the collegiate church, which became Manchester Cathedral, and is the most complete late medieval residential complex to survive in the north west. The collection, assembled to rival the College libraries of Oxford and Cambridge, today numbers 100,000 volumes; many of which were published before 1851.

Above: The chained library of Gorton

Above: West wing of the cloisters
Below: Fox Court, part of the best preserved secular college building in the country. Surviving features to be seen are the baronial hall, cloisters, and dormitories

Left: The Mary Chapel. The Library also has collections of medieval and modern manuscripts, along with a large archive on the history of the Manchester area. Visitors can use tables and chairs dating from the 1650's

Above: The Manchester Evening News Arena was built in 1996. It is the biggest indoor arena in Europe seating 19,500, and has received awards as the world's top indoor arena and the International Venue of the Year

Right: Statue of Robert Owen, by Gilbert Bayes, 1953. Owen was a co-operative pioneer and philanthropist

Below right: Plaque to mark the ballooning exploits of James Sadler, who took his cat along for the flight from a garden behind Corporation Street. Several days later another attempt got him to Pontefract

Opposite page, bottom: CWS offices built between 1905 and 1928. In the background is New Century House (left) and the CIS Tower (right) built 1962, Manchester's tallest building and the highest in Europe at the time of its construction

Victoria Station, opened in 1844. Note the tiled map in one of the entrances showing the old railway company's many routes

Museum of Transport

Exhibits range from horse-drawn buses to the prototype of the first Metro tram. The collection is housed in a former bus depot on Boyle Street and is one of the largest in Britain. There are more than 90 buses here, in the different liveries of North West companies. The first bus service possibly in the world, is thought to have started between Manchester and Pendleton in 1824. The oldest bus here is an 1890 horse-drawn, four-seater vehicle built in Salford for service in Longsight. The Museum also has lots of uniforms, tickets, posters and timetables which help to describe the rise of public transport. Each year a cavalcade of historic vehicles sets off from the Museum to Heaton Park.

Manchester Jewish Museum

Situated in the former Spanish and Portuguese Synagogue, 190 Cheetham Hill Road, the Museum portrays the 250-year history of Manchester and Salford's Jewish community. The ground floor is largely as it was when the building was used for worship (1874-1982). Visitors see the Ark, a cupboard containing the Torah Scrolls; stained glass windows (the one shown below features the seven-branched Menorah and other religious symbols); a Torah Scroll (a handwritten parchment containing the Five Books of Moses); a lamp that burns continuously, and numbered pews. The Ladies' Gallery, upstairs, is now an exhibition area. Included are reconstructions of a Victorian kitchen, with the table set for the Sabbath meal, and a waterproof garment-makers bench.

Omer Board

a shmearer (waterproof-garment makers) bench

a tik (Sephardi scroll)

Manchester University *firsts*

- former student, JJ Thomson discovered the electron

- Ernest Rutherford, the founder of nuclear physics unravelled the structure of the atom

- Niels Bohr worked with Rutherford to produce the theory of the atom's structure

- Lawrence Bragg's team led the world on X-ray crystallography

- An electronic computer, nick-named 'the Baby' which stored a programme and executed instructions, developed in 1948

- Building the world's largest manoeuvrable radio telescope at Jodrell Bank in 1957

- Research students started to use e-mail in the 1970's

- Students' data was moved round the web by 1990

Left: Tower and Council Chamber
Opposite, top: Beyer Laboratories
Opposite: Whitworth Hall

Oxford Road

The University of Manchester is the largest campus in Europe. The buildings in the main quadrangle were designed by Alfred Waterhouse, architect of Manchester Town Hall, and his son Paul between 1874 and 1910.

Manchester Museum (right) is famous for its Egyptology collection - the finds of two Manchester textile merchants in 1890. There are 'mummies' and other artifacts from ancient Egypt, and University pioneering work on the reconstruction of faces of people 3000 years old. Other sections include Zoology, with the huge skeleton of a sperm whale, and the Vivarium with live frogs, snakes and lizards. The Fossils Gallery explores life on earth millions of years ago, including dinosaurs, and the human body is part of the Science for Life interactive display

Above: Fossils Gallery, Manchester Museum

Above: Contact Theatre, Devas Street, reopened in its spectacular building in 1999. Contact specialises in new work which appeals particularly to young people and hosts cutting-edge touring shows. There are also workshops for playwrights, actors and DJ's.

Right and below: The Pankhurst Centre, Nelson Street, was once the home of Emmeline Pankhurst, campaigner for votes for women. There is a reconstruction of her living room where the Women's Social and Political Union was formed in 1903 following the Labour Party's reluctance to press for women's rights. The room features the typewriter used by Sylvia, Emmeline's daughter, and an early version of a walking frame with adjustments for height. Mrs Pankhurst and her family later moved to London to lobby Parliament and in 1928 all women were given the right to vote.

Whitworth Art Gallery

The Gallery has fine collections of British water-colours, engravings and prints, wallpapers, historic textiles and the work of modern artists. There is also sculpture and furniture within the striking exhibition spaces. The gallery and the park were the bequest of Sir Joseph Whitworth, who became a wealthy man through his introduction of uniformity into screw threads.

The 'curry mile', south of the city centre in Rusholme - the largest group of Asian food outlets in Britain

Right: Award winning curry chef at the Royal Naz Restaurant

Platt Hall

The Gallery of English Costume

The gallery has a collection dating from the 17th century to the present day. It also has accessories, early fashion plates and journals and 15,000 photographs illustrating the history of costume since the beginnings of photography. Platt Hall was the 18th century home of the Worsley family and it was bought, along with the estate, by Manchester Corporation in 1908. It became a costume gallery in 1947.

Platt Fields lake

The City of Manchester Stadium

Manchester 2002 Ltd

This stunning stadium was built for the 2002 Commonwealth Games in Eastlands, Manchester at a cost of £110 million. It seats 38,000 and was the venue for the opening and closing ceremonies, track and field events and rugby 7's.

The roof is cantilevered and secured by twelve masts which reach up to 60 metres and is designed to amplify the roar of the crowd. Another special feature is the windows below the roof which open to allow in light and air to dry the pitch.

The seating is being extended by lowering the playing surface by six metres and a permanent stand built on the open end. The stadium will then become the home ground for Manchester City with a 48,000 capacity for the 2003/4 season.

Manchester 2002 Ltd

Above and below left: *The exciting City of Manchester Stadium*

Manchester 2002 Ltd

Manchester 2002 Ltd

The City of Manchester Stadium is the centre-piece of many surrounding new developments. It is part of Sportcity which is the largest sports development to be built in this country. The English Institute of Sport is to have its head-quarters here with training facilities for squash, tennis, badminton and netball, along with physiotherapy and sports medicine services. A new supermarket and shopping centre, restaurants, canal-side homes and an extension of the Metrolink line by the stadium, are all part of the ongoing redevelopment.

Above and below right: The National Cycling Arena at Manchester Velodrome - headquarters of British Cycling

Left: Manchester Aquatics Centre, Oxford Road

Maine Road

Manchester City moved here from their Hyde Road ground in 1923. The new site, a clay pit for brick makers, gave the City the chance to build the biggest ground in England apart from the recently completed Wembley Stadium. There was one stand seating 10,000 and the rest was open terracing comprising of 20 miles of concrete steps.

In the opening game a crowd of 60,000 watched City play Sheffield United in a first division fixture. 76,000 saw a game against Cardiff in the FA Cup later in the season.

There was a record attendance of 84,569 for an English club match, apart from the Cup Final, when they played Stoke City in 1934.

Just after the War, the ground was shared by their neighbours from Old Trafford because of bomb damage. The Platt Lane stand was roofed over and years later seats installed here to make it, at 18,500, the highest number in England.

In 1956 a roof was put over the Kippax Street banking and in the 1960's the cantilevered North Stand (left) was built.

Improvements were made to the Main Stand (bottom) in 1982 and the new Platt Lane End (right) was completed in 1994 with 2 tiers of executive boxes and seating for 6000. The final development was the impressive Kippax Stand (top) with three tiers, 246 boxes and around 11,000 seats.

Old Trafford

United moved here from Clayton in 1910. The ground was terraced on three sides, with a seated main stand. The first game against Liverpool attracted 45,000. The ground could hold 80,000, and a crowd of 70,504 watched a game against Aston Villa in 1920. They did have 80,000 plus crowds but that was at Maine Road while the ground was being rebuilt. The ground record at Old Trafford was for an FA Cup semi-final between Wolves and Grimsby in 1939 with an attendance of 76,962.

United returned to their home ground in 1949 with a game against Bolton. Floodlights were added in 1956 for mid-week European games and the Stretford End was covered in 1959.

A new cantilevered stand was built ready for the 1966 World Cup Finals and this was extended to the open Scoreboard End in 1973. The Main Stand was the next to be cantilevered and then the Stretford End (left) was upgraded.

The North Stand (top) has now been extended, making it the largest in Britain, with the world's largest spanning cantilevered roof, bringing the capacity to 67,000. It is the biggest club ground in Britain and known by Bobby Charlton's description as 'The Theatre of Dreams'. In the East Stand (right) is the club museum which includes a telegram sent prior to the Munich Tragedy by the late Duncan Edwards to his landlady, saying that his flight from Munich had been delayed. Outside the stand there is a memorial clock commemorating the players and officials who died in the 1958 crash, along with a statue of Sir Matt Busby.

Above: Lancashire County Cricket Club, Talbot Road, Old Trafford
Below: Metro tram leaving Pomona station towards The Quays

Trafford Park

Left: Skyhook sculpture by Brian Fell. **Below left:** Trafford Road Swingbridge Plaque, 1892. **Below:** Manchester Docks once had more than 200 cranes. These 3-ton electric cranes became redundant, and in 1988 were dismantled and moved to their present site at the head of the Ontario Basin

Above: *Manchester United's ground from Salford Quays harbour*

Opposite page: *Watersports in the Ontario Basin. Manchester became the third busiest port in Britain with the opening of the Manchester Ship Canal in 1894, but trade declined in the 1970's with changing patterns of trade. The increasing size of container ships meant that the Docks were no longer viable. In 1983 Salford Council purchased the land and have successfully rejuvenated the area now known as The Quays for commercial, residential and leisure developments such as the Imperial War Museum North, The Lowry and The Designer Outlet*

Now, a generation on, the docks are reborn.

The silence fell like smog smothering suddenly everything went dark and the docks died.

Above: Centenary Walkway - local people's reminiscences

The Lowry Footbridge, completed in 2000, links the Lowry to the Imperial War Museum. The bridge can be raised to let shipping through

The Imperial War Museum North

The Museum building was designed by the architect Daniel Libeskind, who worked on the Victoria and Albert Museum and the Jewish Museum in Germany. The design symbolises a shattered globe - a world torn apart by war and pieced together again. The museum is constructed from three shards representing the three areas of conflict - earth, fire and water.

The large exhibits include a Harrier Jump Jet, a Russian T34 tank, a firefighting trailer pump used during the Manchester Blitz, and a 13-pounder artillery gun which fired the first British shell in the First World War.

The Museum also chronicles war in the 20th century from a civilian perspective with sections such as Women and War, propaganda, and many exhibits donated by the public. Images from museum archives project onto floors, walls and visitors. The floor of the main exhibition area is curved to recreate the earth's surface and the pillars are at different angles to represent conflict.

Private Hobday's artificial leg

Above: HMS Bronington - one of the last conventional wooden minehunters of the Royal Navy, berthed in front of the Museum. Bronington was launched in 1953 and ended service in 1988. Prince Charles, who took command of the ship in 1976, introduces an audio tour for visitors

A youngster holding a defused incendiary bomb

A child's dress made from wartime silk escape maps

First World War British Army biscuit

The Lowry

It has been a huge success both in its design and setting and also in the numbers of visitors to see the work of Salford artist LS Lowry, or the other changing exhibitions, along with its two theatres. The Lyric has the largest stage outside London and the Quays Theatre is a smaller version of the Globe Theatre.

Above: Detroit Bridge, formerly a twin-track railway bridge on the line which linked the Docks to Trafford Park. It was floated up the canal to its present position over the Huron and Erie Basins in 1988

Below: The towering North Stand of Old Trafford football ground across the harbour

Left : The Lowry footbridge
Right: Flats next to the Lowry Designer outlet

The Trafford Centre

The Centre, just off the M60, is a popular destination for shoppers, with a wide range of fashion stores, well-known high street names as well as specialist shops in the Festival Village. There is also entertainment with a 20-screen cinema, tenpin bowling, interactive games and turbo bumper cars. The architecture and decor are larger than life, with water features and other surprises. There are lots of restaurants, often in their own themed settings, in the Orient area.

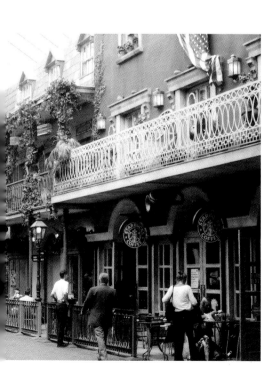

Ordsall Hall Museum is a Medieval timber-framed house built by Alexander Radclyffe in 1512 to replace an earlier cruck hall.

It has an impressive Tudor Great Hall (right), a portrait of a lady in court dress (right below) and the Star Chamber bedroom (right top).

Guy Fawkes is said to have met at the Hall with his co-conspirators before attempting to blow up King James and his Parliament in the famous 1605 plot.

16th century Wythenshawe Hall was the home of the Tatton family between 1540 and 1926. A frieze, found behind 18th century panelling, celebrates a marriage between the Tatton and Booth families in the fourteenth century. The estate was bought by Lord Simon of Wythenshawe, who presented it to the city

Below: Heaton Hall was built in 1772 for the Earl of Wilton. It is one of the best examples of neo-classical homes in Britain, set in 600 acres of parkland. The interior is magnificent, including the circular dressing room of the Dowager Lady Egerton, featuring eight mirrors and arches trimmed in gold leaf. In the Hall's library is a picture of one of the regular horse races held at the park in the 19th century. The races ceased because of the crowds' drunken and riotous behaviour and moved to Aintree. So the early races at Heaton Park were the forerunner of the Grand National. Down by the lake is the facade of Manchester's old Town Hall, which stood on King Street and was re-erected here in 1912. Old trams run on certain days from the Middleton Road entrance and there is a walled garden in the wooded area west of the Hall.

Left: Fletcher Moss was a local alderman and he bequeathed his house and gardens to the public in 1919. The botanical rock garden is particularly impressive with winding paths, a pool, rare plants and waterfalls. In a cafe overlooking the gardens there is a plaque recording the efforts of a group of local ladies, who met here to campaign against the fashion for Egret feathers which threatened the bird with extinction. Their efforts led to the founding of the Royal Society for the Protection of Birds in 1889.

Greater Manchester
...and beyond

Above left: Great Budworth, near Northwich: one of Cheshire's prettiest villages

Above right: Paradise Mill, Macclesfield Silk Museums

Right: Anderton Boat Lift, near Northwich, known as the 'Cathedral of the Canals', built in 1875

Above:

Whit Friday Band Contest, Saddleworth

Below:

Dobcross, Saddleworth

Standedge Tunnel, on the Huddersfield
Narrow Canal at Marsden,
is the longest, deepest and highest
above sea level in the country

Left: Dovestones Reservoir, Saddleworth

Top left: Hartshead Pike, built in 1863
Top and below right: Mottram in Longdendale village
Above left: Tameside Canal Festival, held each July

Top: Portland Basin Museum, Ashton
Far left: Tameside Canals Festival, Ashton
Left: Fairfield Moravian Settlement, established in 1785
Below: Werneth Low - from here there are spectacular views as far as the Welsh hills; sunset and glowing light panoramas of the Manchester region

Lyme Park Stockport

Left: Lyme Hall is Elizabethan, with alterations carried out in the 1730's. It is well known for its Grinling Gibbons woodcarvings, Mortlake tapestries and clock collection

Below left: The Orangery, built in 1862

Below middle: Lyme Cage - built in the 1520's possibly as a watch tower. It may have been used to detain poachers. The present structure was built in the 18th century

Below: Whaley Bridge Wharf, Derbyshire, on the Peak Forest Canal. This was the terminus of the Cromford and High Peak Railway, which was famous for the inclined planes and slopes along the route

Canal-side minstrel at the Wharf

Top: Kinder Reservoir and Kinder Sc···
Above: 1932 Kinder Trespass plaqu···
Hayfield
Left: Hayfield
Right: Millennium Bridge, New Mil···

Left: Hat Museum, Wellington Road North, Stockport. The only museum in the UK dedicated to the world of hats and hat making

Below: Tudor style Bramall Hall was the home of the Davenport family. It was opened to the public in 1936 and has important 16th century wall pictures drawn with vegetable dyes

Right: Air Raid Shelters, Chestergate, Stockport, preserved as they were in 1943 when the air-raids began to recede and the shelters closed

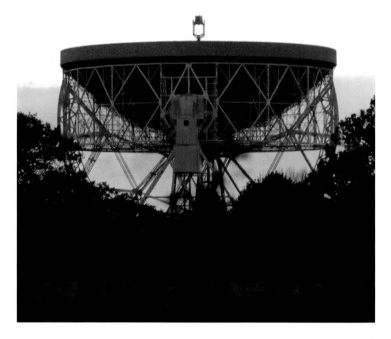

Opposite:
Top: Alderley Edge
Below left: 17th century
school house, Nether Alderley
Below right: Jodrell Bank, site
of the world famous Lovell Radio
Telescope and also a science centre,
planetarium and arboretum

This page:
Top: Prestbury
Left: Hare Hill walled Gardens,
near Prestbury
Right: Norman Chapel, Prestbury

Quarry Bank Mill

Top: The Mill was founded by Samuel Greg in 1784 to harness the water power of the River Bollin.

Left: The world's most powerful 50 ton working Mill Wheel. This was originally at a flax mill in Yorkshire but is similar to the Mill's 1818 Hewes wheel

Below: The Village Shop was run on a co-operative system so that profits were shared and the workforce had cheap, fresh food

Left: Mill demonstrator with
a Lancashire Loom in the
Weaving Shed
Top: Mill entrance and
worker's cottage
Above: The Mill weir provided
a five acre reservoir of power

Tatton Park

Top: Bridge in Japanese garden
Below and right: The Gardens

Opposite:
Top: The Hall, owned by the Egerton family for nearly 400 years, is a treasure house of glassware, paintings by Canaletto and Van Dyck, porcelain, and Gillow furniture
Bottom: Tatton Mere

Knutsford

Opposite
Top: May Day dancing on the Heath
Middle: May Day sand drawing
and procession.
Bottom: The Moor Pond

This page:
Left and below: The Tower was erected
in memory of Mrs Gaskell in 1907
by Richard Harding Watt
Above top: Princess Street
Above: Marble Arch, King Street

165

Top: Lymm - the 17th century cross approached by steps cut into the rock
Left: The Bridgewater Canal at Lymm

Top, right: Arley Hall gardens - the double herbaceous border which was first laid out in 1846. The Hall is the home of Viscount and Vicountess Ashbrook and has been owned by the same family for over 500 years

Right: The Golden Gates, Warrington, were shown at the 1851 Great Exhibition and brought from Ironbridge in 1893 by a local councillor who was also the director of a foundry

Dunham Massey

Opposite

*The estate, near Altrincham, was
bequeathed by the 10th Earl of Stamford
to the National Trust in 1976.
The Hall is mainly18th century and has
a noted collection of Huguenot silver*

This page

Bottom: *Restored Elizabethan Water Mill,*

Left and below:

The lake at Sale Water Park was created through the excavations to build the embankment for the adjoining motorway

Right:

Worsley, the birthplace of British canals. James Brindley completed the Bridgewater Canal in 1761 to take coal into Manchester. The water discoloration is caused by the iron ochre which still leaks out from underground tunnels

Lark Hill Place -
a reconstructed
street at
Salford Museum
and Art Gallery

Astley Green Colliery
Tyldsley, closed in 1970.
It is now an industrial
museum operated by the
Red Rose Steam Society.
There is an impressive
steam winding engine,
which was the largest
machine ever used in the
Lancashire coalfields

Wigan Pier

Trencherfield Mill - the world's largest
original working steam engine

'The Way We Were' Heritage Centre,
including the Palace of Varieties
and Victorian Classroom

The Museum of Memories

Opposite page:
Pennington Flash - the largest area
of water in Greater Manchester.
Popular for watersports and birdwatching

Left: Smithills Hall and gardens, Bolton, dating from Medieval times

Below: 'Model village' - Barrow Bridge, Bolton, with 63 steps to help workers to the mill but now a route to the moors

Right: Halli'th Wood, Bolton, is a late medieval mansion where Samuel Crompton invented the Spinning Mule in 1779, which transformed the cotton industry from a cottage-based enterprise to a factory-based process

Right, below: Last Drop Village, Bolton

Left: A replica of Liverpool Castle lies on the banks of Rivington Reservoir. Rivington Pike tower, built in 1773, is on the moor top. The woodlands are part of Rivington Country Park, once the estate belonging to Lord Leverhulme, the Bolton business man who made his fortune from the production of soap

Below: 14th century Turton Tower, once the home of Humphrey Chetham - founder of the School named after him in Manchester

Bottom: The Pigeon House, Rivington Country Park

The East Lancs Railway runs for 8 miles between Bury and
Rawtenstall and reopened as a preserved line in 1987. **Above:**
Ramsbottom Station. **Left:** Approaching Brooksbottom Tunnel.
Left below: Engine driver and station master at Ramsbottom

Right: Black puddings, the local delicacy, are
sold on Bury Market. The World Black Pudding
Throwing Championships are held each
September at the Corner Pin Pub in Ramsbottom

Left: Peel Tower, erected in 1852 in memory of Bury born Sir Robert Peel - Prime Minister, repealer of the Corn Laws and founder of the first police force

Near left: Clock tower in Bury town centre

Below: Irwell Valley Sculpture Trail near Ramsbottom - the UK's largest public art scheme, stretching 30 miles from Salford Quays to Bacup

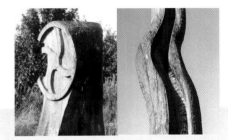

 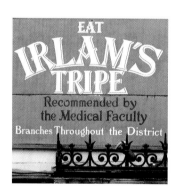

Above: *Rochdale Pioneers Museum - the building where 28 workers established the first co-op shop to produce good food at reasonable prices in 1844*

Right: *Alfred Waterhouse tower, on the imposing Gothic Town Hall*

Healey Dell Nature Reserve

The 1841 Whitelees beam engine at Ellenroad Engine House, Milnrow, which also houses the massive working mill steam engines - Victoria and Alexandra

Hollingworth Lake, built in 1804 to supply the Rochdale Canal, has always been a great visitor attraction

The Royal Exchange from the Shambles

Urbis from Cathedral Gardens

Acknowledgements

Thanks to: Don Rainger - Manchester Jewish Museum, Chris Saville - Printworks, Danielle Shields - John Rylands Library, Vanessa Walters - Royal Exchange Theatre, Museum of Transport, Manchester Cathedral, Pankhurst Centre, St Ann's Church, Penny Haworth - Whitworth Art Gallery, David Green - Manchester Central Library, Lisa Hill - Stockport Museums, Manchester Craft and Design Centre, Emma Marigliano - Portico Library, Melanie Hamer - Wigan Pier, Ellenroad Engine House, Red Rose Steam Society, Salford Museum and Art Gallery, Manchester Council, Royal Naz Restaurant, Opera House, The Triangle, Val Smith - Manchester Museum of Science and Industry, Midland Hotel, Affleck's Palace, Circus Tavern, Britannia Hotel, Contact Theatre, The Trafford Centre, Midland (Crowne Plaza) Hotel, Peter Mellor - Manchester Cathedral Visitor Centre, Ian Farrow - Cafe Pop, for their permission and co-operation for the photography.

Thanks to: Michael Powell - Chetham's Library, Father Denis Clinch and Bryan Clarke - St Mary's Church, Duncan Broady - Greater Manchester Police Museum, Duncan Craig - People's History Museum, Sue Hibbert - MEN Arena, Manchester Museum, Lisa Hawkins - Palace Theatre, Ann Flenley, Phil Sayer - Imperial War Museum North, Len Grant, Kim Gowland and Tracey Walker - Manchester Art Gallery, Trevor Hollingworth - East Lancashire Railway photographs, Caroline Hill - Quarry Bank Mill (The National Trust), Jonathon Webb - Webb Aviation, Manchester 2002 Ltd, Macclesfield Silk Museums and to anyone I may have inadvertently missed, for generously supplying photographs and information.

Special thanks to Judith Warrender, Cynthia Hollingworth and Peter Haddington for their suggestions and diligent proof reading and to everyone who gave me permission to include them in photographs, and for their patience.

Further reading

Manchester by Clare Hartwell, Pevsner Architectural Guides, Penguin Books, 2001
The Mancunian Way edited by Jane Price, Clinamen Press, 2002
City Life Guide to Manchester edited by Jonathan Schofield, City Life, 2002
Free Days Out in the North West by Peter Haddington, Wharncliffe Books, 2002
Manchester Town Hall Guide, Willow Publishing, 2002
Discovering Manchester guides, Manchester-at-Leisure Ltd

Further information
Check with the venue or a Tourist Information Centre for times of opening and admission details.

The author Keith Warrender lives in Timperley. He is a designer and photographer and publishes books and postcards on Manchester and surrounding areas.